AMAZING MILITARY FACTS

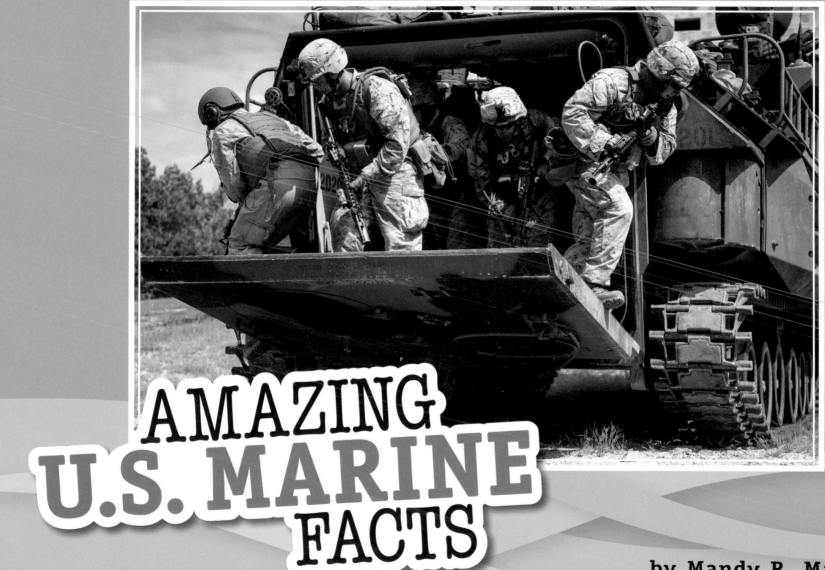

AMAZING U.S. MARINE FACTS

by Mandy R. Marx

CAPSTONE PRESS
a capstone imprint

Pebble Plus is published by Capstone Press,
1710 Roe Crest Drive, North Mankato, Minnesota 56003
www.mycapstone.com

Library of Congress Cataloging-in-Publication Data
Names: Marx, Mandy R., author.
Title: Amazing U.S. Marine facts / by Mandy R. Marx.
Other titles: Amazing United States Marine facts
Description: North Mankato, Minnesota : Capstone Press, 2017. | Series:
  Pebble plus. Amazing military facts | Includes bibliographical references
  and index. | Audience: Age 4-8. | Audience: Grades K-3.
Identifiers: LCCN 2016016903| ISBN 9781515709541 (library binding) |
ISBN 9781515709862 (pbk.) | ISBN 9781515711216 (ebook (pdf)
Subjects: LCSH: United States. Marine Corps—Juvenile literature. |
  Marines—United States—Juvenile literature.
Classification: LCC VE23 .M3915 2017 | DDC 359.9/60973—dc23
LC record available at https://lccn.loc.gov/2016016903

Editorial Credits
Kayla Rossow, designer; Jo Miller, media researcher; Kathy McColley, production specialist

Photo Credits
Shutterstock: Oleg Zabielin, 23, 24; U.S. Marine Corps photo by Chief Warrant Officer 2 Jorge A.
Dimmer 3d MAW COMCAM, 5, Cpl. Alan Addison, 11, Cpl. Chris Stone, 1, Cpl. Ryan Mains, 9,
Lance Cpl. Aaron S. Patterson, MCBH Combat Camera, 21, Lance Cpl. Antonio Rubio, 17,
Lance Cpl. MaryAnn Hill, 7, Staff Sgt. Ezekiel R. Kitandwe, 19, Sgt. Steve H. Lopez, cover;
U.S. Navy photo by JO2 Zack Baddorf, 13, MC2 Tamara Vaughn, 15

Note to Parents and Teachers

The Amazing Military Facts set supports national curriculum standards for science related
to science, technology, and society. This book describes and illustrates amazing facts about
the United States Marine Corps. The images support early readers in understanding the
text. The repetition of words and phrases helps early readers learn new words. This book
also introduces early readers to subject-specific vocabulary words, which are defined in the
Glossary section. Early readers may need assistance to read some words and to use the Table
of Contents, Glossary, Read More, Internet Sites, Critical Thinking Using the Common Core,
and Index sections of the book.

Printed and bound in the USA.
009655F16

Table of Contents

Amazing Marine Facts

A military plane crashed

in an enemy country.

Who does the U.S. government call?

The Marines! They get ready to go

at a moment's notice.

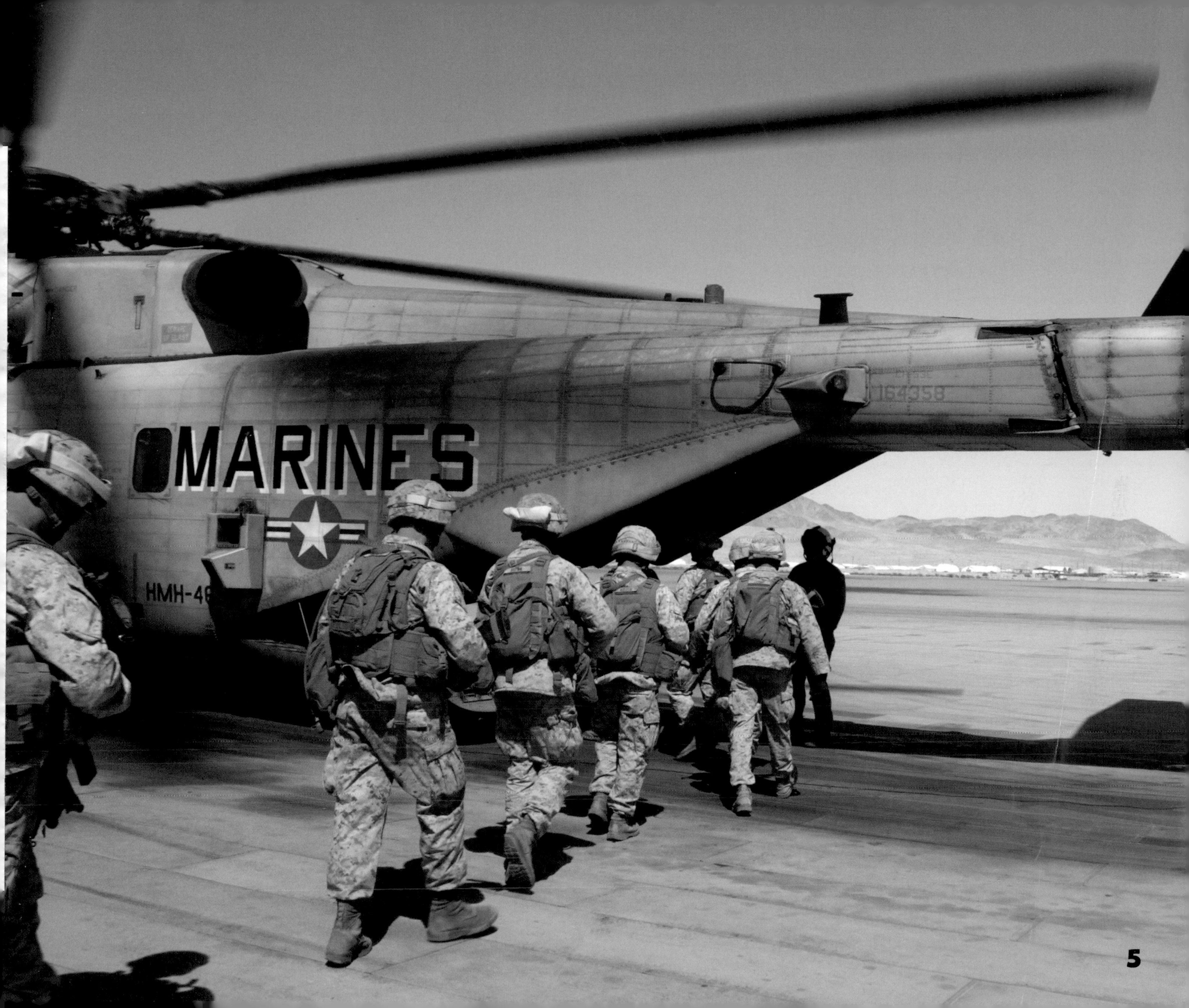
MARINES
HMH-46
164358

Amazing On-the-Job Facts

Marine recruits train for 12 weeks. Their final test is the Crucible. It lasts 54 hours. Recruits march 48 miles (77 kilometers) as part of the test.

The smallest Marine task force is a MEU. It has 2,000 Marines. They can be ready to fight in just six hours.

Marines help all around the world.

An earthquake hit Haiti in 2010.

Marines delivered 57,368 meals

to people there. They brought

589,764 bottles of water.

Amazing Vehicle Facts

Tanks move on land. Ships move on water. But the AAV-7 vehicle does both. It can move 21 Marines from ship to shore.

The AH-1W is an attack helicopter.

It protects Marines on the ground.

It fires missiles, rockets, and a gun.

The helicopter also has strong sensors.

They track enemies.

The Osprey takes off like a helicopter.

But it flies fast like an airplane.

It can hold 24 Marines.

Amazing Weapons Facts

Marine snipers aim carefully.

They fire M40A5 rifles.

Snipers hit targets 0.6 mile

(1 km) away. That's longer than

10 football fields.

The M777 Howitzer is a strong cannon. It can hit targets 19 miles (30.5 km) away.

Glossary

cannon—a large, heavy gun that usually has wheels and fires explosives

earthquake—a very strong shaking or trembling of the ground

helicopter—aircraft that can take off and land straight up and down

missile—an explosive weapon that is thrown or shot at a distant target

recruit—a soldier in training

sensor—an instrument that detects changes and sends information to a controlling device

sniper—a soldier trained to shoot at long-distance targets from a hidden place

target—an object at which to aim or shoot

task force—a group formed for a limited period of time to deal with a specific problem.

Read More

Alpert, Barbara. *Military Amphibious Vehicles.* Military Machines. North Mankato, Minn.: Capstone Press, 2012.

Gordon, Nick. *U.S. Marine Corps.* Epic Books: U.S. Military. Minneapolis: Bellwether Media, 2013.

Jones, Keisha. *My Brother is in the Marine Corps.* Military Families. New York: Powerkids Press, 2016.

Internet Sites

FactHound offers a safe, fun way to find Internet sites related to this book. All of the sites on FactHound have been researched by our staff.

Here's all you do:

Visit www.facthound.com

Type in this code: 9781515709541

 Check out projects, games and lots more at **www.capstonekids.com**

Critical Thinking Using the Common Core

1. Why would military weapons need to hit targets as far away as 19 miles (30.5 km)? (Integration of Knowledge and Ideas)

2. When might the Osprey be the best aircraft to use for a mission? (Key Ideas and Details)

Index